EATING OUR WAY THROUGH THE ANTHROPOCENE

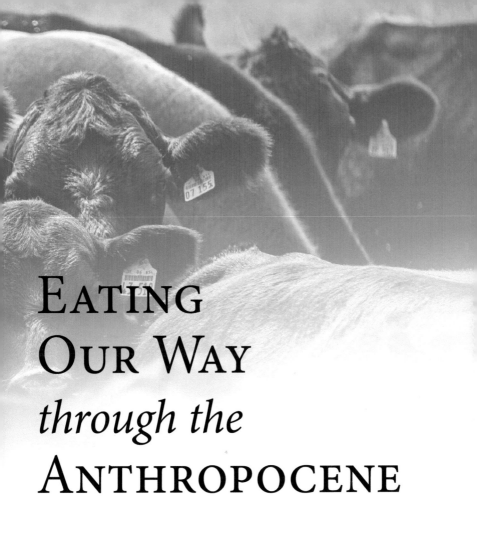

EATING
OUR WAY
through the
ANTHROPOCENE

Jessica Fanzo

THE UNIVERSITY OF UTAH PRESS
Salt Lake City

Publication of this keepsake edition is made possible in part by
The Wallace Stegner Center for Land, Resources and the Environment
S.J. Quinney College of Law
and by
The Special Collections Department
J. Willard Marriott Library

This lecture was originally delivered on March 18, 2020, at the 25th annual symposium of
the Wallace Stegner Center for Land, Resources and the Environment.

The Defiance House Man colophon is a registered trademark
of The University of Utah Press. It is based upon a four-foot-tall Ancient
Puebloan pictograph (late PIII) near Glen Canyon, Utah.

ISBN: 9781647691035 (paperback)
ISBN: 9781647691042 (ebook)
CIP data for this volume is available from the Library of Congress.

Cover and frontispiece photo by Etienne Girardet on Unsplash.

Foreword

The Wallace Stegner Lecture serves as a public forum for addressing the critical environmental issues that confront society. Conceived in 2009 on the centennial of Wallace Stegner's birth, the lecture honors the Pulitzer prize–winning author, educator, and conservationist by bringing a prominent scholar, public official, advocate, or spokesperson to the University of Utah with the aim of informing and promoting public dialogue over the relationship between humankind and the natural world. The lecture is delivered in connection with the Wallace Stegner Center's annual symposium and published by the University of Utah Press to ensure broad distribution. Just as Wallace Stegner envisioned a more just and sustainable world, the lecture acknowledges Stegner's enduring conservation legacy by giving voice to "the geography of hope" that he evoked so eloquently throughout his distinguished career.

The 2020 Wallace Stegner Lecture was delivered by Professor Jessica Fanzo from Johns Hopkins University on the subject of "Eating Our Way through the Anthropocene."

Robert B. Keiter, Director
WALLACE STEGNER CENTER FOR LAND,
RESOURCES AND THE ENVIRONMENT

This lecture is centered on the role of food systems as both victims and instigators of climate change. I first define the Anthropocene and then discuss food systems and diets during this period. I discuss some of the ways in which diets, which are born out of food systems, are changing and how they contribute to and are also impacted by climate change. Ethical questions will be considered, namely, "Can we have it all?"—Can we have both human and planetary health as priorities and outcomes of the global food system?

The Anthropocene defines Earth's most recent geologic time period as being human-influenced, or anthropogenic, based on overwhelming global evidence that atmospheric, geologic, hydrologic, biospheric, and other Earth system processes are now being significantly altered by human beings. The term *Anthropocene* was coined in the 1970s and has generated both scientific and political momentum around understanding and mitigating the human footprint on the planet.[1] Recent papers and reports have talked about the Anthropocene as the sixth extinction,[2] highlighting issues around planetary health[3] and the role of human-induced climate change.[4]

We are now at an interesting point in the world. The 2018 report by the Intergovernmental Panel on Climate Change (IPCC) argues that the world will look very different when we hit 1.5°C warming from preindustrial temperatures, which we will reach in the next fifteen years. Avoiding that 1.5°C warmer world will require "rapid, far-reaching, and unprecedented changes across all aspects of society."[5] We are talking not only about mitigating climate change— we are talking about an everything change. Everything that we do is starting to be and will be different with climate change, and climate change has far-reaching impacts for everyone across every aspect of society.

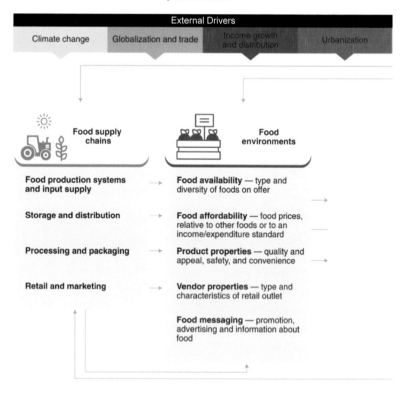

Figure 1. Food Systems Framework. (Source: Jessica Fanzo et al., "The Food Systems Dashboard Is a New Tool to Inform Better Food Policy," *Nature Food* 1, no. 5 (May 2020): 243–46, https://doi.org/10.1038/s43016-020-0077-y).

In 1992, a group of scientists issued a warning to humanity: they predicted other changes to Earth's systems beyond temperature change, including warming and rising carbon dioxide (CO_2) emissions that would lead to multiple detrimental impacts on natural resources and the planet overall.[6] Twenty-five years later, another group of scientists reviewed the latest climate research and asked whether these scientists were right in their predictions.[7] With respect to most of the indicators, including freshwater resources decline, total deforestation, increase in dead zones, and decline in vertebrate species abundance, the predicted changes turned out to be true. What is more alarming is that the pace of change across these indicators has accelerated in the last two decades. The pace

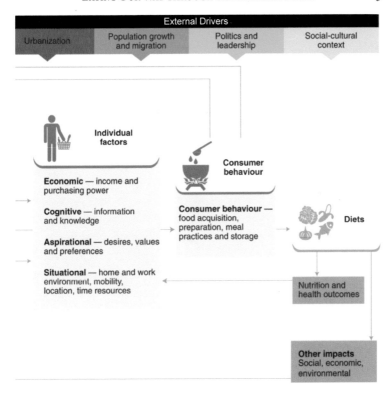

at which we have lost forests, biodiversity, and species, and the increase in temperature and greenhouse gas emissions accelerated over the last decades, which rings alarm bells for humanity.

THE ROLE OF FOOD SYSTEMS

To contextualize the discussion, I introduce a framework of food systems developed by the UN High-Level Panel of Experts on Food Security and Nutrition (HLPE) that convened in 2017.[8] This framework provides an overview of food systems, their sectors, and influencers.

Food systems are made up of supply chains, starting with agriculture and food production systems; food is stored, distributed, processed, and packaged; it moves to markets and other food environments, which is the place where we as the consumers make choices of what to buy or to order. Consumers bring individual factors: willingness to pay, knowledge, aspirations, and desires, as well as issues of distance from the market and time available. The market and the food environment also influence individual decisions, along with what kind of foods are available, their cost, product properties (quality, branding, or organic labels), types of vendors (an organic market, a farmers' market, or a corner store), and the advertising (a buy one get one free deal), among many other signals that influence decisions of consumers of what they want to buy. While some signals are quite perverse, and others beneficial, these factors seek to direct consumers, influence behaviors and diets, and thus influence the plethora of outcomes of food systems. My work focuses on nutrition and health outcomes of the food system, but there are many other sociocultural, economic, and environmental outcomes. There are also many exogenous drivers that influence, shape, and transition these dynamic food systems. Climate change, urbanization, population pressure, trade policies, subsidy policies, and politics all influence the food system in different ways.

We have seen an acceleration in the pace of global food system transformations: the land used for agriculture has grown over the last few decades and is now plateauing at around 40 percent of arable land use for agriculture; beef production has been increasing; pesticide and fertilizer use have also been on the rise. The food system has been changing in both positive and negative ways, and we know that food systems are contributing to the changing climate.[9]

Roughly 40 percent of the Earth's land is used for food production. Nearly a quarter of the global greenhouse gas emissions come from agriculture, and that's only at the production side of food systems. Around 25 percent of those emissions come from cows (ruminant enteric fermentation produces methane, a potent greenhouse gas), but other contributors include transportation to move meat, waste, manure, and energy use. Rice production also produces a considerable amount of methane, and there are greenhouse gas emissions from the production of fertilizers.[10]

As food moves along supply chains or value chains, there are vulnerable points for the impacts of climate.[11] Issues of food safety, transportation and storage, marketing and retail, and food prices have not been completely modeled across the entire supply chain, but some can be highlighted. Modeling future scenarios of agriculture production in a 3°C warmer world, the quantity of crops is going to change—the types and yields of growable crops will vary.[12] The global South is particularly affected by declining yields, while places in the north, such as Canada, are going to do quite well in a 3°C warmer world. Overall, there is a trend for declining crop yields, making a 3°C increase a dire one to live in.

When examining water resources in the context of a convergent climate scenario (in which there is aggressive economic growth but a "business as usual" mitigation strategy towards climate change), it is possible to see exacerbated water stress in the border of the Sahel in sub-Saharan Africa, in South Asia, and in the Middle East.[13] It will become even more difficult to grow the types of crops needed to feed the world. Comparing a climate change scenario to a business-as-usual (as is) scenario, there is an imminent threat of species extinction in many parts of the world, with sub-Saharan Africa and South America being hardest hit.[14] Biodiversity is under pressure from both climate change and agricultural expansion. Conservative action to address and mitigate climate change would grant some protection, but the threat of species loss remains high.

There will also be declines in the nutritional quality of crops due to a CO_2 fertilization effect—one in which we have higher amounts of CO_2 in the atmosphere due to global warming. These include declines in the content of zinc, iron, and protein across wheat, rice, soybeans, maize, and some other major crops.[15] While studies have focused on the impact of elevated CO_2 levels on three important nutrients across major crops, the full range of potential nutrient loss across a wider range of crops is unknown and severity is likely to depend on where these crops are grown. This points to the idea

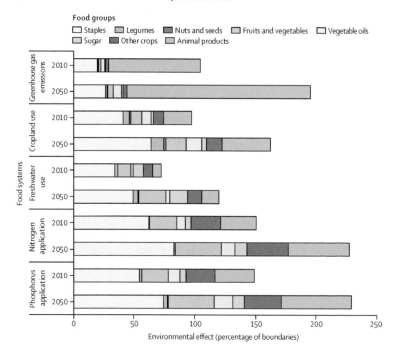

Figure 2. Environmental effects in 2010 and 2050 by food groups on various earth systems based on business-as-usual projections for consumption and production. (Source: W. Willett et al., "Food in the Anthropocene: The EAT-Lancet Commission on Healthy Diets from Sustainable Food Systems," *The Lancet* 393, no. 10170 (February 02, 2019): 447–92, doi:S0140-6736(18)31788-4. With permission from Elsevier).

that the quantity of crops produced is not the only impact of climate change; food quality is also at risk.

Food safety will continue to be a major food system concern. Aflatoxin is a mycotoxin that can contaminate peanuts, maize, and sometimes rice and is particularly problematic in sub-Saharan Africa. Aflatoxin exposure has many detrimental health impacts including liver cancer and some associations with stunted growth in children. In one study, current aflatoxin contamination levels were compared to those in a 2°C and a 5°C warmer world and found that the European Union will have a devastating aflatoxin contamination issue of several major crops, including maize, in a warmer world.[16]

The EAT-Lancet Commission (2019) report gathered data on the impact of different food groups on environmental indicators (including greenhouse gas emission, land use changes, water footprint, nitrogen, and phosphorus applications) at present-day and in 2050 in a business-as-usual approach (Figure 2). They found that animal products have a significant greenhouse gas footprint, but other crops can also have large environmental footprints. For example, fruits and vegetables can require high nitrogen application and result in considerable water and phosphorus application footprints. Staple grains and tubers also have an environmental footprint across these five environmental indicators.[17] Since 50 percent or more of these staples are being fed to animals that we then consume, the resulting footprint of animal products is multiplied. When considering environmental impacts of food, it is important to consider how, where, and by whom these foods are grown. Tomatoes grown in a hothouse are very different from tomatoes grown in an urban garden. Cows are not the only enemy in the food world—there are other foods with high environmental footprints. It is also important to consider environmental footprints beyond greenhouse gas emissions. Unfortunately, animal source foods do have a significant footprint on the planet, as they demand large amounts of land, require fertilizer use that contributes to feed, and emit large amounts of greenhouse gases.

OUR DIETS IN THE ANTHROPOCENE

The way in which we eat matters not only as an outcome of the food system. We all eat every day: it keeps us alive, and it also helps us thrive. Food brings us together, and it plays a central cultural role in society. For some, it's an inherent part of their livelihood—many Indigenous peoples center their life around food production. Diets are an important measure of the health of the food system.

Data from the Burden of Disease project show that most diets around the world are suboptimal.[18] Figure 3 shows estimated global intake data (in gray) and regional and sub-regional intakes (in

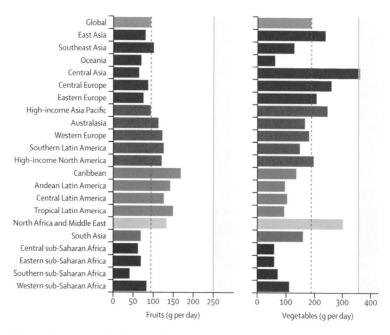

Figure 3. Age-standardized intake of dietary factors among adults aged twenty-five years or older at the global and regional level in 2017. (Source: Ashkan Afshin et al., "Health Effects of Dietary Risks in 195 Countries, 1990–2017: A Systematic Analysis for the Global Burden of Disease Study 2017," *The Lancet* 393, no. 10184 (May 11, 2019): 1958–72, https://doi.org/10.1016/S0140-6736(19)30041-8). Reprinted with permission.

different colors). The five bar graphs on the first row show healthy components of a diet (fruits, vegetables, legumes, whole grains, nuts, and seeds), while the bottom five show the less healthy components of a diet (red meat, processed meat, sugar-sweetened beverages, trans fats, and sodium). The shaded green areas show a recommendation of what we should strive to consume. Globally and sub-regionally most people are not eating enough vegetables (except for Central Asia) or legumes (except for Latin America and sub-Saharan Africa), and no region is meeting the recommendations for fruits, whole grains, nuts, and seed consumption. Looking at the less healthy parts of our diets, we see that many people meet or exceed the recommended intake of red meat (e.g., the United States) and processed meats (Asia, Latin America, and the European

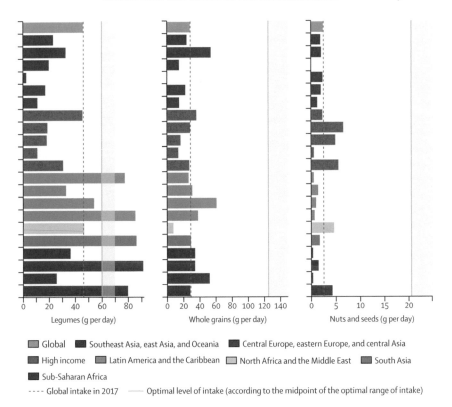

| Legumes (g per day) | Whole grains (g per day) | Nuts and seeds (g per day) |

☐ Global   ■ Southeast Asia, east Asia, and Oceania   ■ Central Europe, eastern Europe, and central Asia
■ High income   ☐ Latin America and the Caribbean   ☐ North Africa and the Middle East   ■ South Asia
■ Sub-Saharan Africa
---- Global intake in 2017   —— Optimal level of intake (according to the midpoint of the optimal range of intake)

Union). Every region of the world is well over the recommended consumption for sugar-sweetened beverages, sodium, and trans fats—which if consumed in high amounts can be detrimental for human health.

These trends in changes in consumption have resulted in a massive global malnutrition burden. One in three people are malnourished and without concerted action in the next ten years one in two will be malnourished. Approximately 800 million people go to bed hungry, and that number has been rising for the last three years after significant declines over the previous fifteen years.[19] There is a reversing trend in the progress against hunger and malnutrition. The Food and Agriculture Organization (FAO) of the United Nations argues that this increase in hunger is due to conflict

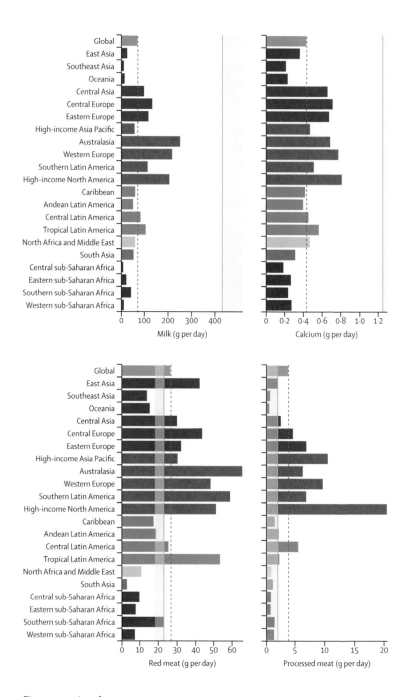

Figure 3. continued.

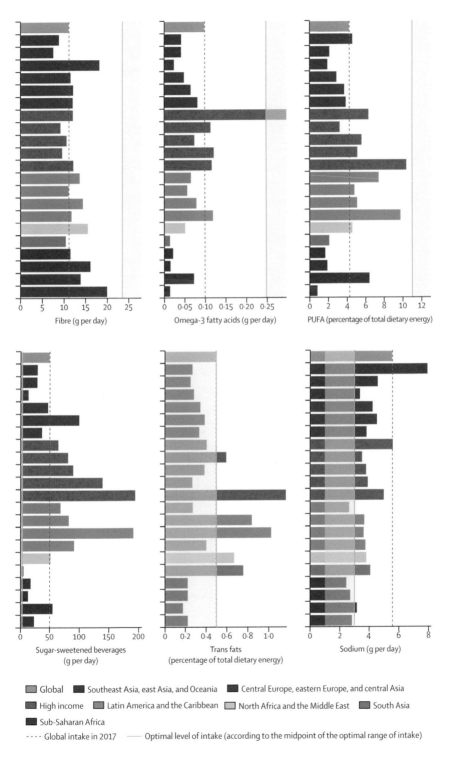

Fibre (g per day)

Omega-3 fatty acids (g per day)

PUFA (percentage of total dietary energy)

Sugar-sweetened beverages (g per day)

Trans fats (percentage of total dietary energy)

Sodium (g per day)

☐ Global ■ Southeast Asia, east Asia, and Oceania ■ Central Europe, eastern Europe, and central Asia
■ High income ■ Latin America and the Caribbean ☐ North Africa and the Middle East ■ South Asia
■ Sub-Saharan Africa
- - - - Global intake in 2017 —— Optimal level of intake (according to the midpoint of the optimal range of intake)

and climate change. There are 150 million children who are physically underdeveloped or chronically undernourished, and they'll be cognitively impaired for life without action in their first five years. That corresponds to nearly 25 percent of the world's children under the age of five, and the negative impacts are debilitating for individuals, families, and for countries. Around 50 million children are acutely malnourished.[20] Seasonal hunger, famines, and conflicts all contribute to these children being at a high risk of mortality. Forty million children under the age of five are overweight—and this is rising exponentially along with adolescent obesity. Over 2.1 billion adults are overweight or obese, resulting in a massive and costly burden to society.

Diets are not only a large contributor to this malnutrition burden, but they are also the top contributor to death and disability—more than air pollution and more than smoking.[21] Diets that are meant to nourish us are now killing us. High intakes of sodium and sugar and low intakes of whole grains, fruits, nuts, seeds, and vegetables are the biggest contributors to death and disability now in the world. Most people are dying from non-communicable diseases such as cardiovascular disease, diabetes, and cancers. We've shifted from communicable to non-communicable diseases, and that trend is increasing in low- and middle-income contexts as well as in high-income ones. There is a significant and growing burden of under-nutrition, overweight, and obesity in low- and middle-income countries.[22]

A potential solution to this complex problem is the EAT-Lancet healthy reference diet, which became rather controversial for recommending a diet significantly low in animal-source foods. The goal of the EAT-Lancet commission was to define a healthy diet that would allow the world to stay within Earth's planetary boundaries while feeding a global population of ten billion humans by 2050. There are significant inequities in who gets access to what type of diet: high-income countries are consuming too much animal-source foods such as meat and dairy—way beyond what is needed to meet dietary needs—and these diets have been having impacts on the climate, natural resources, and ecosystems. Other places in South Asia and parts of sub-Saharan Africa consume diets well within the planetary boundaries and for some populations, they are not meeting their dietary needs. These countries and populations are making insignificant contributions to climate change but will suffer more from high-income dietary decisions.[23] There's a real inequity of who eats what, who produces it, and who will be impacted by climate change in more severe ways.

Interesting ethical questions underline this conversation. There are places in the world, the United States being one example, that have energy-intensive lifestyles and energy-intensive diets, which contribute significantly to human health costs and to climate change disruption.[24] However, it is the economically poor households who disproportionately suffer the impacts of climate change. In sub-Saharan Africa, South Asia, and East Asia people are being forced to move or migrate, despite not being the ones who are consuming excessively or eating in environmentally intensive ways. This begs the question: do we have the right to eat wrongly?

Access to healthy diets is unequal around the world. Work examining the cost of animal source foods around the world shows that in low-income countries animal source foods are more expensive due to insufficient supply chains and inability to trade perishable foods. For example, eggs are very difficult to trade and incredibly expensive for low-income households in low-income countries.[25] Americans pay 10 to 15 percent of their total income for food, which is low compared to other places in the world such as Bangladesh, Nigeria, and Rwanda, where 60 to 70 percent of total incomes are spent on food. A study showed that 1.6 billion people on the planet cannot afford the proposed EAT-Lancet healthy and sustainable diet, even if it is low in animal source foods, which are expensive.[26] If the EAT-Lancet diet were to include larger amounts of animal source foods, it would be unaffordable for a larger share of people.

There are ethical issues around meat production amidst hunger. As early as the 1970s, Frances Moore Lappe's book *Diet for a Small Planet* argued that the environmental footprints of animals are

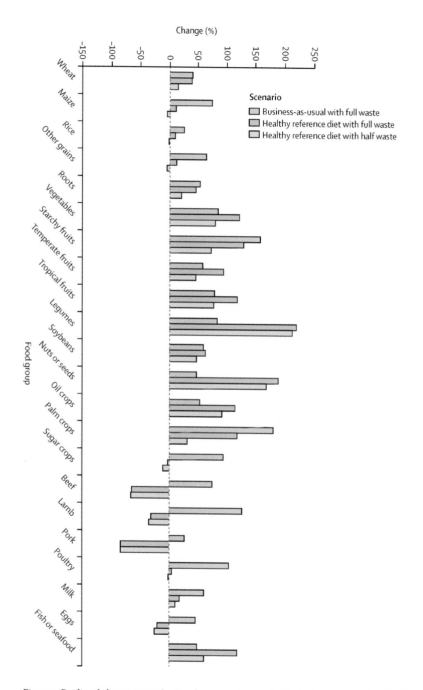

Figure 4. Predicted change in production from 2010 to 2050 for the business-as-usual with full waste scenario and the healthy reference diet with full or half waste scenarios. (Source: W. Willett et al., "Food in the Anthropocene: The EAT-Lancet Commission on Healthy Diets from Sustainable Food Systems," *The Lancet* 393, no. 10170 (February 02, 2019): 447–92, (doi:S0140-6736(18)31788-4). With permission from Elsevier).

intensive, and cows are particularly resource-intensive: they use large amounts of energy, water, and feed compared to other animal foods like chickens or fish.[27] Is it right for half of the global cereal production to become livestock feed when we still have so many people who cannot meet their basic caloric needs? It is a question of competing priorities: is that the right way to use the limited land on this planet?

The EAT-Lancet commission projected the impacts of dietary shifts to a flexitarian, healthy and sustainable diet, while also cutting food loss and waste in half by the year 2050 (Figure 4). They found that the food production systems would have to change to meet the needs of this different diet between current production and 2050. There would be no increase in the production of whole grains or cereals, which is very different to how most agriculture subsidies and research and development are structured around the world. Production of vegetables and fruits need to increase by 75 percent and 50 percent, respectively.[28] There would need to be at least a 50 percent increase in fish production, with a large portion of that increase being from aquaculture since wild marine resources are also over-sourced. Legumes and nuts would have to increase by 75 percent and 150 percent, respectively, and currently the varietals of nuts to be able to produce for that increase in yield have not been identified. The most controversial part of the EAT-Lancet is that red meat production would have to decline by 65 percent, which has significant implications on livelihoods of ranchers and cattle farmers. Another study shows the current global supply of vegetables does not support the recommended consumption of 400 grams of fruits and vegetables daily. That is also the case for fruit and vegetable production projections into the year 2050, with the supply of fruits and vegetables not meeting basic needs.[29]

Can we have it all? Can we have human health, improve diets, and stay within planetary boundaries to save ourselves and save the planet?

What options do we have that are ethically permissible and socially acceptable? As consumers, we live in confusing times.

Alternative proteins such as Beyond Meat, Impossible Burgers, and lab-grown meats present potential options. Some cultures regularly consume insects as a source of protein while others find it disgusting. Consumer acceptance of different options will become intractable issues (akin to concerns with genetically modified organisms [GMOs]) during a time of rapidly changing food options.

One of my team's projects investigates ethically permissible options for altering beef production and consumption practices in the United States. We asked consumers in Nebraska and California to place foods in groups—Americans will typically group foods similarly to the Dietary Guidelines for Americans: meats, eggs, dairy, vegetables, pizza, and mac and cheese. The few foods most respondents were unable to group were plant-based milk, impossible burgers, and in-vitro burgers. Consumers in the United States were unable to group these new alternative protein products as they did not really know how to make sense of them or how they compare with the foods they know.[30]

Can we have it all? The answer is: it depends.

First, we need massive food systems transformation. All the recent major food- and climate-related reports reinforce that tinkering around the edges is no longer an option. We are at a point when we need to significantly transform food systems to ensure that everyone gets access to a healthy, sustainable diet.

Second, we also need countries to create and implement coherent food systems policies. While most countries have agriculture strategies, dietary guidelines, and nutrition policies, not one country has a holistic food system policy that sets priorities for agriculture, nutrition, health, climate, and biodiversity. There is a need for government action around holistic food system policies, and for governments to think about food as an entry point to better health, better economic development, education, cultural and social cohesion, a sustainable planet, conservation of natural resources, and of course national security.[31] Food systems can be the sweet spot for health, environment, and economies, and can help harmonize policy goals for oceans, trade, health, finance, and business.[32] Food can be seen to improve multiple policies within a country.

A third recommendation is to keep the food system within environmental limits. A more plant-based diet or flexitarian diet has a significant impact on greenhouse gas emissions, but sustainable food production technologies and cutting food loss and waste will play a big role in curbing increases in land-use change, water use, and eutrophication, or nutrient spill-over into waterways.[33] We need to make use of different approaches and tools to keep food systems within planetary boundaries.

Fourth, there is a need for both mitigation and adaptation to climate change within food systems. There are innovative mitigation and adaptation strategies including improvements in crop management, livestock management, climate services on farms, improved supply chains, changes in consumer demand and dietary shifts, and stopping food waste. These can come with co-benefits for livelihoods, biodiversity, and health, and have the potential for both mitigation and adaptation.[34] There are multiple options that, if paired with political will, investment, and policies, could produce significant changes in the environmental footprint of food systems.

Fifth, we need to help consumers navigate these complex issues. Even as a nutritionist, I am often confused by the nutrition information available. We desperately need to understand what is navigable and usable for consumers—from practical tips and solutions to big conceptual notions such as a sustainable diet, a healthy diet, and environmental footprints of different foods.[35] Chile recently implemented front-of-the-package warning labels on foods high in sugar, salt, and fat, which help consumers navigate around unhealthy foods in an easier way. Chile took it one step further in that they regulated these foods—they cannot be sold in schools or advertised on TV in the hours that children would typically watch television. A study showed a 25 percent reduction in purchases of these unhealthy foods with warning labels on the front of the packages. Consumers need more of those kinds of tools to be able to make decisions in currently complex food environments. Lastly, we also need an enabling political environment for food systems transformations. Governments need to care about food policies, and there needs to be supportive political environments. Donors need to invest in food systems—there is a real underfunding of nutrition programs and projects at a global scale. Civil society needs to continue pushing governments to act and hold the private sector accountable. We also need academia and research to continue to build this evidence base that's now emerging and to govern the conflicts of interest that keep arising in the nutrition space. Across the food system, the private sector has significant power, which creates a power imbalance. We need governments to take control and to shepherd their food systems in the directions that their citizens deserve.

Notes

1. Paul J. Crutzen, "Geology of Mankind," in *Paul J. Crutzen: A Pioneer on Atmospheric Chemistry and Climate Change in the Anthropocene* (New York: Springer Cham International Publishing, 2016), 211–15, https://doi.org/10.1007/978-3-319-27460-7_10.
2. Lancet Planetary Health, "A Sixth Mass Extinction? Why Planetary Health Matters," *Lancet Planetary Health* 1, no. 5 (August 2017): e163, https://dx.doi.org/10.1016/S2542-5196(17)30083-9.
3. W. Willett, et al., "Food in the Anthropocene: The EAT-*Lancet* Commission on Healthy Diets from Sustainable Food Systems," *The Lancet* 393, no. 10170 (February 02, 2019): 447–92, doi:S0140-6736(18)31788-4.
4. Sandra Díaz, et al., "Pervasive Human-Driven Decline of Life on Earth Points to the Need for Transformative Change," *Science* 366, no. 6471 (2019), https://doi.org/10.1126/science.aax3100.
5. Intergovernmental Panel on Climate Change (IPCC), *Global Warming of 1.5°C. An IPCC Special Report on the Impacts of Global Warming of 1.5°C Above Pre-Industrial Levels and Related Global Greenhouse Gas Emission Pathways, in the Context of Strengthening the Global Response to the Threat of Climate Change, Sustainable Development, and Efforts to Eradicate Poverty,* 2018.
6. Union of Concerned Scientists, *1992 World Scientists' Warning to Humanity,* https://www.ucsusa.org/resources/1992-world-scientists-warning-humanity.
7. William J. Ripple et al., and 15,364 scientist signatories from 184 countries, "World Scientists' Warning to Humanity: A Second Notice," *BioScience* 67, no. 12 (December 1, 2017): 1026–28, https://doi.org/10.1093/biosci/bix125.
8. Jessica Fanzo et al., "The Food Systems Dashboard is a New Tool to Inform Better Food Policy," *Nature Food* 1, no. 5 (May 2020): 243–6, https://doi.org/10.1038/s43016-020-0077-y.
9. Willett et al. "Food in the Anthropocene," 447–92.
10. Tim Searchinger et al., *World Resources Report: Creating a Sustainable Food Future: WRI,* 2018.
11. Jessica Fanzo et al., "The Effect of Climate Change Across Food Systems: Implications for Nutrition Outcomes," *Global Food Security* 18 (September 1, 2018): 12–9.
12. Searchinger et al., *World Resources Report.*
13. Searchinger et al., *World Resources Report.*

14. Roslyn Henry et al., "'The Role of Global Dietary Transitions for Safeguarding Biodiversity," *Global Environmental Change* 58 (September 1, 2019): 101956.
15. Samuel S. Myers et al., "Increasing CO2 Threatens Human Nutrition," *Nature* 510, no. 7503 (June 5, 2014): 139–42.
16. P. Battilani et al., "Aflatoxin B1 Contamination in Maize in Europe Increases due to Climate Change," *Scientific Reports* 6, no. 1 (2016): 24328.
17. Marco Springmann et al., "Options for Keeping the Food System within Environmental Limits," *Nature* 562, no. 7728 (October 2018): 519–25, https://doi.org/10.1038/s41586-018-0594-0.
18. Ashkan Afshin et al., "Health Effects of Dietary Risks in 195 Countries, 1990–2017: A Systematic Analysis for the Global Burden of Disease Study 2017," *The Lancet* 393, no. 10184 (May 11, 2019): 1958–72.
19. Development Initiatives, 2018 Global Nutrition Report: Shining a Light to Spur Action on Nutrition, Bristol, UK, 2018.
20. Food and Agriculture Organization, International Fund for Agriculture Development, United Nations Children's Fund, World Food Program, and World Health Organization, *The State of Food Security and Nutrition in the World 2018—Building Climate Resilience for Food Security and Nutrition*. Rome, Italy, 2018.
21. Afshin et al., "Health Effects of Dietary Risks," 1958–72.
22. Barry M. Popkin, Camila Corvalan, and Laurence M. Grummer-Strawn, "Dynamics of the Double Burden of Malnutrition and the Changing Nutrition Reality," *The Lancet* 395, no. 10217 (January 4, 2020): 65–74.
23. Willett et al., "Food in the Anthropocene," 447–92.
24. *Los Angeles Times* Editorial Board, "Editorial: Wealthy Countries Are Responsible for Climate Change, but It's the Poor Who Will Suffer Most," *Los Angeles Times,* September 15, 2019, https://www.latimes.com/opinion/editorials/la-ed-climate-change-global-warming-part-2-story.html.
25. Derek D. Headey and Harold H. Alderman, "The Relative Caloric Prices of Healthy and Unhealthy Foods Differ Systematically Across Income Levels and Continents," *The Journal of Nutrition* (July 2019), https://doi.org/10.1093/jn/nxz158.
26. Kalle Hirvonen et al., "Affordability of the EAT–Lancet Reference Diet: A Global Analysis," *The Lancet Global Health* 8, no. 1 (January 2020): e59-e66.
27. Youfa Wang et al., "Trends and Correlates in Meat Consumption Patterns in the US Adult Population," *Public Health Nutrition* 13, no. 9 (September 2010): 1333–45, https://doi.org/10.1017/S1368980010000224.
28. Willett et al., "Food in the Anthropocene," 447–92.
29. Daniel Mason-D'Croz et al., "Gaps between Fruit and Vegetable Production, Demand, and Recommended Consumption at Global and National Levels: An Integrated Modelling Study," *The Lancet Planetary Health* 3, no. 7 (July 2019): e318-e329, https://doi.org/10.1016/S2542-5196(19)30095-6.

30. Elizabeth L. Fox et al., "A Focused Ethnographic Study on the Role of Health and Sustainability in Food Choice Decisions," *Appetite* 165 (October 1, 2021): 105319, https://doi.org/10.1016/j.appet.2021.105319.

31. Dariush Mozaffarian et al., "Role of Government Policy in Nutrition—Barriers to and Opportunities for Healthier Eating," *BMJ* 361 (2018): k2426, https://doi.org/10.1136/bmj.k2426.

32. Kelly Parsons and Corinna Hawkes, *Connecting Food Systems for Co-Benefits: How Can Food Systems Combine Diet-Related Health with Environmental and Economic Policy Goals?* European Observatory on Health Systems and Policies, (Copenhagen, Denmark, 2019), https://www.ncbi.nlm.nih.gov/books/NBK545695.

33. Springmann et al., "Options," 519–25.

34. Cynthia Rosenzweig et al., "Climate Change Responses Benefit from a Global Food System Approach," *Nature Food* 1, no. 2 (February 2020): 94–7.

35. International Food Information Council (IFIC) Foundation. *2018 Food and Health Survey.*

ABOUT THE AUTHOR

 Jessica Fanzo is the Bloomberg Distinguished Professor of Global Food Policy and Ethics and vice dean of Faculty Affairs at the Nitze School of Advanced International Studies (SAIS) at Johns Hopkins University. She is the editor-in-chief for *Global Food Security* and since 2017 on various advisory groups including the Food Systems Economic Commission, the Global Nutrition Report, the Global Panel of Agriculture and Food Systems for Nutrition Foresight 2.0 report, the UN High-Level Panel of Experts on Food Systems and Nutrition, and the EAT-Lancet Commission. She is the author of *Can Fixing Dinner Fix the Planet?*, published by Johns Hopkins University Press in 2021.